Broken Prose, Spoken Poems

Second Edition

Free verse by
Clifford Schrage

**For my writing students
who've come to love
the finest words
set in their finest order.**

Copyright 2019 by the author

ISBN 978-1-987852-23-3

Published by Wood Islands Prints; 670 TCH Rte 1; Wood Islands PE C0A 1R0; Canada

The author can be reached via email at
sherryandcliff@gmail.com
Copies of this book can be purchased from the author and are also available at amazon.com

Cliff Schrage is a high school creative writing, film studies, and literature teacher. He is a father of eight (six adopted) and grandfather of four. His novels include A Fruitful Field *and* Silas Dillon Of Cary County, *and his poetry has appeared in various periodicals in North America. He makes his home on Long Island, New York; and in the summer he resides on Prince Edward Island, Canada.*

COYOTES

We never see you, you elusive canine knaves,
diminutive wolves,
coy cousins of conquered pets,
committers of murders,
moon shadow chasers,
gang members hiding from light taking
night's quiet by her throat in long crescendos of cries,
pup yips, whelp barks, snarls,
howling wails pitched high as whistles—
social celebrations over bloody kills.

We never see, but ever hear
these suffused pitches, your singing of
"a land of darkness and the shadow of death."
At the food chain summit and summer's quiet gloom
you howl wails pitched high as whistles
heard in the nether east of Eden,
stealing serenity, taking her by the throat in
this fallen world. Your frenzy of a dozen dialoguing voices
startles the stillness in stars at the treetops of the universe,
stills faint pulses of contiguous creatures
in your bloody desperation, your
desperate despair—
like humans in their social loneliness
in this fallen world.

SWANS

As sallow, ashen angels
these lean fowl fly
beneath clear heavens
in the lavender evening.

Saintly over a smooth waveless surface
as ancient ships in white canvas,
silent on an indolent inlet
they drift, sail.

Nothing flutters
or shifts
in moments of moving time
until the swans'

Wings widen,
slam air under necks stretched forward;
webbed feet slap across a surface of water
in the lumbering dusk.

This sound swallows silence
in sudden turbulence;
the swans launch, softening their noise,
lifting upward, rising toward heaven

in vast white flight.
All earth's fixed
this moment—with this flock's motion
and is still.

SHARON, VERMONT

This is the other side of the world
Where dairy cows remain docile,

Dressed in panda bear clothes, bashful—
Grazing in daisy-dappled, green walls of pastures,
Ascending.

Dusk descends on talons,
And clouds are mountains in white and gray, or
Cumulus peaches enthroned over walls of emerald
    green.
White River is yellow-silver while this slow dusk
Descends.

We begin to drop into sleep, drowsing into
That place where time is sly—
The sound of still crickets slow dancing
With humming chime of moving water,
Both alone.

When dawn rises,
One red barn yawns,
Demanding all the attention.
On the other side of the world
Dusk descends.

ACROSS THE RUBBLE OF BABEL

They see us across the water—

Publics of another culture.
Uniting is strained.
For centuries a band of water separates us.

They see us beneath evening darkness,
Across the rubble of Babel

And water.
Lights flickering—

We see them—
Flickering lights.

Our hands, feet, the way we eat, fight, live—
Like them for centuries.

Two sides. Us and them,
We and they, couplets—

They see us. We see them—
Lights flicker

NOVEMBER

In the Michigan village
By the lake at the base of the hill
Fat turkeys wrestle fat hands,
Stern human eyes.

Stout axe to oak stump, cold steel to soft throats—
Folks watch and mock;
Birds run amuck in blood,
Drop dead, headless.

Under enormous barren elms
Old folks stroll streets. others indoors peer out
    windows.
In the market the butcher weighs the farmer's work
On a balance scale.

Crimson, gold, and yellow leaves
Have fallen to huddle to curbs and fences,
Fallen into brown,
To wither to mulch.

HERMITS

Hermits live in these hills,
Nomads on these roads.
Who will go? Who will reach them?
We saw the far forsythias splattering yellow paint,
And the white poplars popping open on the
    perimeters of fields
Early in silver spring.

We're fat,
Prone on a raft in a pool, cool,
Hands clasped behind head,
Cigar in jaw,
Eyes closed,
Facing heaven, sleeping.

Harvest fields burst with whiteness,
Chasing, calling laborers.
Who will come before winter?
Hermits live in these hills,
Nomads on these roads.
Who will go? Who will reach them?

LONG ROAD

The road creeps slowly on its belly
Portland to Fort Lauderdale,
Tail to tongue.

We hear the ocean's baritone voice in broken cadence
Murmuring songs through hours of soaring owls,
See its slow dance with the moon.

We enfold the coast in the cushioned world of this car
Passing acres and acres of sea,
Wishing...wishing... with the ocean, praying.

THE OTHER SHORE

Flow river, over velvet sands,
Around serrated boulders
Broken in the valley.

Slither river, like the serpent
Under and over the
Mountain's foot.

Live river, move with
Rushing, laughing motion in
Darkness.

Rise high river, fall headlong
Coursing with breathing buoyancy
After cloudburst.

Let us, river, cross over assured,
Leaving silver here to golden banks that glisten
The other shore.
The amber and emerald green cedars point like
    spires
Toward heaven.

AFTER A STORM

Around root clusters of trees,
Sunken logs,
Rusted shopping carts,
Cinder blocks, bald tires, junk men have dumped;

Broken Prose, Spoken Poems

Sticks and leaves float swiftly eastward
Toward the tide of Forge River.

Here behind the market you bend over the soft moss
    of this stream bank.
After the storm sunlight breaks, water still falling
    from bare Limbs
Above you.

Small plants under currents bend gilded green.
Sand ripples, loosening minute roots.
Tiny westbound minnows suspending in emerald
    midwater,
Are forced backward, then jolted forward, inches
    farther west.
In pure unsullied strength—
With no show of strain—
As though their tiny minds had will,
These slight fish find their way beside the bank
In a cove with little current
For rest.

Here you hear a shuttering song of one bird stirring
    solitary.
Here you hear the market's racket afar, the roar of
    the highway farther,
This tranquil water moving beside you.

A primordial voice opens your inner ear.
You listen, rising and returning—
Back to the racket, back to the roar, into your
    current.

KNOLLS

Wobbly rocking knolls filled with yellow in autumn,
Where verdant green cedars point toward heaven—
Let's walk there awhile
In the shining—
Over there, over yellow lawns,
Over rolling knolls, into the yellow autumn.
Let's amble around in the emerald and gold where

AUTUMN SWAMP MAPLE

Look far down Brown's River, see
The swamp maple—all orange
Among tupelos and cattails.

Once you trudged through thorns and marsh,
Found this tree,
Climbed its branches.

Each leaf held many colors—
Rose, sunflower, and sunrise
Over summer green.

NEW YEAR'S DAY

In the frozen pile of the snow plow's push
Chunks of curbside ice sit
Like stones in
Russet speckles in white sand.
Someone shuffles warily to the corner.
A whole year has fallen like a parcel
Into the mailbox
huddled in South Dakota coldness—
Empty, alone, blue.

LAST SEASON

Last season you left us, sailing off for heaven.
Eighty days. This vacant space
Has made so great a pain.

We peer across the street through two panes of glass,
Witness they've cleared trees to
Emptiness.

Few oaks still standing stand exposed in space,
Slim with thin limbs of green stretching into
Barrenness.

It will be many summers
Before restored in fullness.
Last season you left us, sailing off for heaven.

RECESSES OF A SUMMER

They hide in high black grass,
In dark green garden stalks,
Under the high hay stacks,
And cry through night, grieving
Beneath attentive stars.
We hear them—sorrowful,
Sad crickets.

And the moon, too, mourns,
Waning with tears
That pour
On old slabs of
Broken slate
Which lead the way we once walked.

IN THE HEART OF A HEATWAVE

In the heart of a heatwave
Of a Long Island summer,
We keep from heat in shadows of trees,
And sleep in the music of leaves,

Worn with the sweat of our souls
In blue viscous air,
We turn the earth with the shovel of hunger.
The Spirit hears our appeals and pleas

Watching over while
His wind lifts walls of haze
Between us away.
In sodden evening,

Under the roaring of thunder,
Safe from the quaking of the deep,
We awaken from tombs of our sleep.
In dew-covered morning

Calm on the shore after rain,
With the chorus of waves at the sea—
We walk together
Chained to the rhythm,

In the heart of a heatwave
Of a Long Island summer.

DECEMBER WINDOW

Outside this window
The long gusts of wind whimper;
Winter tilts a gray face
To the earth.

Steady rain,
A lone swallow slips on the air to a tree limb,
Pauses, shakes twice,
Flies away.

LATE SPRING DOGWOOD, NEW JERSEY

In afternoon
A softened muffled wind,
A ripple of water, red-white petals in the air
Drop on the top of the pond.

Dusk, still wind,
Stars drip on the still water surface.
One cricket sings.
A dogwood weeps.

THREE DUCKS

April's hills are teal and wet,
Dripping gray rain filling valley pools.

Bars of sunlight break, shattering
Shining glistening fragments over all that held gray.

Three ducks fly over Terrel River,
Calling, quaking calm silence.

THE PRODIGAL

I mourned the day you left.
Gray sky, winter, still gull on a wharf post;
The horizon line blended into blurred mingling—
Sky and sea,
Uncertain confusion,

Ambiguous mist.
I watched your ship sail eastward
Inching toward Murray River,
Smaller and smaller.

NOTHING EVER CHANGES

Blue jays scream; neighbors sleep.
Early morning's
Sun's blue hands hold you, and
The flow of cold water falls into soil
From the water can in your hand.

Like a child with cotton candy you carry upright
Lavender and lilac blossoms.
Water showers, mist leaps,
Light frames a rainbow—

Early May morning.

These remind us—nothing ever changes,
That our lives remain stable, still eternal.
Behind you in the high locust limbs the lofty air blows and moves
Swiftly as angels with scathing swords, flinging fragrance,
Tossing beige blossoms.

Stiff, sinuous, tapered limbs lean forward.
Pushes and brushes of breezes from the sea press against trees
And you; greenness lilts.
New buds of evergreens open in
Yellow palms of hands, and worship.

I watch you, my wife, your ardent movement as
You shine through lucid breakfast glass in green
    honesty.
Hair lifts behind you, shining aglow against white
    cotton
Contrast like petals of cherry blossoms
Against pastel expanse of sky.

Noon will come; the petals will fall, and summer will
    come.
Life will intrude with its revolution,
Its flurries of spores, organisms,
Sore hearts and old scores,
But nothing ever changes.

DARK HOUR

A dark hour prowls forward.
Winter limbs scribble shadows,
Wave naked shapes in the wind.

Thick limbs *creak*
One lonely word over and over
Against a page of sky.

Cold, subtle flurries of snow
Fall. Dark barks of a fox rove
Over the low silence.

Jesus, You are the huge spruce,
While she at peace hides
Like a grouse in a bough.

CHRISTMAS NIGHT

Out for wood
I find the birches whiter by moonlight.
All's quiet, light, still and
Full with stars.

Inside
Voltage beams, mumbles, hums;
This moon finds no place,
This night no thought.

I'd like to stay, pray,
Or write a poem;
But it's cold and I'm only
Out for wood.

MIDNIGHT

It's midnight, April, a quiet hour.
You've come alone to this blackness,
The edge of black woods.

Rainfall's drained. Pools and streams swell.
Water drips from still trees—
No blossoms, leaves, buds.

White clouds crack, split.
Blackness fills the cracks. Stars blemish blackness.
Small light from a window reaches out its warm
    hand.

The sounds that voice within blackness:
Peepers in the forest mere,
Ducks of the duck farm, dull hum of the Atlantic,

A car's wheels on a far rain soaked street,
Barks of worn dogs,
This dripping, your breathing.

You've come alone to escape your strapping wrestler,
    wakefulness;
Alone to escape your sleeping home, alone to meet
    with your forgiver
In the light of this raucous blackness.

CLOUDS OF DAWN, WYOMING

The clouds of dawn march on the mountains.
They come synchronized, banging broken drums
While fingers of wind
Strum the strings of willows.

Swiftly water courses in the valley
Are filling and flowing with water,
While time, never flinching,
Cunningly rushes to some indifferent surface.

Noon shadows in vigilance
Languish in the meadows.
Sycamore twigs sharpen shadows
On green-black ground.

And all afternoon
The lucent face of the sun on swollen pools
Beams as the moon's
In night's peak.

PAINTING A HOUSE

On a Sunday I see from this roof
Puffs of blue smoke from cold mufflers:
Family cars leaving for church.
In the still of the distance the sea lies in sapphire,
A span of marsh land, cattails shining like ice,
December dry.

I recall Grampa's white hair,
Red weathered face urging, "Go to school. Become a doctor.
Become a lawyer."
He'd lean down, muss my hair, smoke cigars,
Coloring homes with cumbersome brushes,
Youthful blue eyes like the sea.

A quiet tide swirls, revolves.
Cold wind blows and shrills like violins in my ear.
Starlings dance over dead crabs, cluster like bees, leave ruffled.
Another thought, another shingle,
The melody of bells tolling in the village—
Months have drifted since I've visited God's house.

I blow breath through the narrow tunnel of my fist,
Slide down with palm and heels, slowly,
So careful not to spill blue on this roof;
I approach the tops of the ladder rails

Welcoming like open arms—
The safety of level ground.

VERMONT CEMETERY

Ice nestles in tire scars crossing grassy pastures.
Cold approaches early here—
As autumn throws gold on the ground.
It is dawn. Barn doors yawn. Steeples stretch.
Venus shines in violet skies.

We stroll behind this old church
Down a slope beneath maples
Where names and years of lives engraved
In slabs of stone like wheel scars in earth
Make rows and rows.

There's zeal that spears with jealousy holding back
    the plague;
That whips, that drives the animal out, turning
    tables,
A zeal that burns with burning fire,
That scars, marred more than any man's,
That cries to one creator.

A crow *caws*, flutters.
Tame wind blows cold up the slope.
Dead, brittle leaves rustle
Clustered like netted fish
Against the slender rows of stones.

ARMS

It's graceful the way
The gray clouds climb
Carried by hands of wind
Over the ocean coast through stars
In the darkening far fields of the universe.

They're kept in the power of the wind,
As offspring in arms of a Father,
Not knowing the course,
Not knowing the cost,
Or where.

TREE FARM

At dawn songs of birds float across the tree farm.
Swallows dive
Down,
dart along the rows of yews, junipers, azaleas in
　　scarlet orange.
A dim moon blemishes a blue sky.
One young doe within the openness—still, bright—
Rests in the first light of sun, grazing, gazing across
This place that is always filled with thick stillness,
Drowsing summer mists, winter frosts.

Once you searched here,
Lost in listening, longing to stay while
Sounds of storms swept inside your soul.
There are things that no eyes have seen, no ears have
　　heard,
No understandings have understood—
things prepared for any who'll love
unforbidden fruit.

Now, in clamorous storms far from here
you find inside your soul
these summer mists, winter frosts, rows, swallows,
　　fawns,
this tree farm, repose.

TENSES

The moon's shining washes this present tense.
Its crescent rays bathe Moriches Bay
Whose waves paint the shore boulders white
And gray
Again and again.

The moon had joined us in the past
Perfect. It had been invited
Full and close
As it had risen over wide open spaces in
Trees, between houses, hills, clouds,
Possessing the purple nights.

The future moon will wane again, will covertly
Hide, will
Seep, smear, cover, rise,
Fall, will even become blood—not only in some
    poem—
But right here,
While the future perfect will have strode
Over Moriches Bay.

GREEN EYES

Thawing earth softens, swells,
Slips off thickness of winter—
Melts and strips this quilt of snow—sliding slowly
As though earth legs kick it
To the foot of the hill.
We sit before new glass at this window.
Gray driving rain chases wind
To corners, Moody Blues' music resonates

Carrying us back forty years.
Grassy holes disclose themselves through snow—
Green eyes peeking from frozen sleep
Through blurry windows of slush

DAYS

The days of oak buds pass by.
They shiver open, exploding over
Shadows of trees breathing.

Those early oak leaves wait in white
Like the feet of the unborn—
Fresh, unstained spaces.

In a moment shade lifts as sunlight
Shifts behind high clouds. The sound of wind
Dies, or sings acres away.

We talk of autumn, and see that we
Like oak leaves had walked over fields, so far,
Hiding behind tales.

We've tumbled out into light,
Humbled, aware that
The days of oak buds pass by.

BRIDE

His eyes long to look upon his bride
more than all the color of the world,
Her wreath is sweet, fragrance sweeter
Than the favored season's breezes.
Her embrace like desert freshets
quench him.

His heart longs for hers.
She shines as light from sun.
He hears the supple sound of her voice.

Someday they'll enter gates, step on salient streets,
hand in hand in hallowed happiness,
in great white rays of light.
Their music—hers in His—
the harmony of stars
as they approach, closer.

AFTER THE HURRICANE

The tide drowned the docks and high spiles,
And ducks just stepped onto grass.
We brought our bags of bread and fed the brown
Females, the green feathered males.

The wind wafted the heavy haze of September.
The sun fell red in the west
melting with yellow smudges
In trees across Orchard Neck Creek.

The power in town tarried all windy night.
The crickets of Moriches: thick, black,
big as frogs—
Gossiped in the gloom.

All along the southeast shore
In the wind pummeled, limb pummeled homes,
candles burned.
Some men slumbered when the light returned.

YELLOW MAPLES

What was once a place of darkness
On a day as bleak as this is, is
Now a place of lavish light beneath canopies of
    trees—
Spacious sugar maples whose limbs like summer
    bride's maids' are brown,
Wearing gowns of powerful yellow,
With trains at bare root-feet

spread on autumn's floor in yellow.
Poised inside like a bride,
Stands the slender fir posing in blue-evergreen
Holding a cluster bouquet of honey suckle vine,
Rising with quiet smiles
On her autumn wedding day.

These maples—yellow chatter,
singing the song of starlings
Deep within their hearts and throats.
Dark clouds come to darken;
these yellow maples brighten. Thunder comes
    tumbling
And windy rains pour and blow these

Starlings out from under these trees, and
Graceful thousands over green fields fly in formation.
They take their song, their dancing,
Leaving the sound of dull falling rain.
As rain still falls these tall maids cry.
As darkness falls, this blue bride sighs.

ICE STORM IN NEW YORK

The clock woke us to that ice storm,
Alarming the dark dawn to the cold. We were
Glad the yellow bus refused to roll over the icy roads,
That school would close all day.

Soon with the music of the first act
The sun burst, shoving aside cold rain curtains;
Then with the music of the second act
We came gazing in wonder at bright wet shining.

All glazed, dripping, clicking, sparkling sunburst,
The trees thought they looked best:
tall leafless ones wore radiant halos;
Birches nearly broken bent as birches do;

But the evergreens were beaten, bowed
Down with broken boughs, slumped like drunken
    men
Over fences, ice laden—hanging limbs
Swinging like arms in wind.

Such a menace of violence and crime:
We had our cameras at the scene.

FLORIDA SONNET

These clouds eclipse the sun out of our sight.
A gust! And now and then our sense can smell
A sudden glimpse which does not want to light.
It hides in hills of clouds that also tell
Of days at noon with breaks and open space
Which widen into whiter starry nights
That drip a silver gaze and heaven's trace

Like oranges, sweet oranges from heights.
These clouds eclipse the moon into the dark
Like fruit in limbs that hide within the shade
As we with thirst await beside the bark
For ripeness to come, for blossoms to fade.
It's the swollen, full fruit of sagacity
That falls like light with calm alacrity.

OCTOBER HOUR

Sunless clouds lower.
Mounds of moss bulge above dead leaves
And needles—Soft springy cushions
Entangling roots of oak and pitchpine.
These are traces of jade
left to suggest last summer.

We pace. It is balmy.
We think we hear one weak cricket
in the middle of this woodland, somewhere
under what's rotting
speaking her words, somewhere.
We strain

with the sane same
patience we take when we shake out a last drop,
to listen, and wonder if we imagine,
Longing for all that remains
of the late stages
of summer.

NIGHT OF A NEW MOON

I'm walking before a night of a new moon.

Winter is over the island,
dead wind and cold oak limbs
Above old hard snow on the dirt road.

I go alone, sleepy,
like the slow sun falling over the duck sheds.
I come to the field by the fishpond
Where water under ice creaks and gurgles
and snow dust swirls in the air.

Two moons ago
Goldenrod shone in the grass.
Earth and sky
Now drowns in winter dusk.

I go home slow
To hear in sleep
Sweet music in my skull
In a dark night
Of a new moon.

MAGIC

Magic
Things like huge majestic doors opening
On thin hinges; plump penguins submerged, flying
    fast
Through freezing currents;
Like ponderous polar bears on water frozen
Over northern Manitoba;
like a man abiding
Forty years in God's forge—
Forged strong, sturdy.
Magic

Like the avalanche launched
Descending like white flocks
Falling to its place of rest.
Magic.

I DREAMED YOU DIED

I stroll this street as
sleepless as three stars that
still pace the lanes of last night's rouse, lingering,
falling west.
In the east a green glow grows higher,
Gleaming brighter.

I dreamed you died.
I saw you gallop off
gallantly riding a white steed, deep into night, intent
toward a red crescent moon,
far on some unseen horizon line.
I thought you glanced back once.

I dreamed you died, and I grieved
leaping back into childhood grieving
rides we'd never taken,
crescent moons we'd never pursued,
horizons too far, too late, or too tired,
over all we wished could be.

You seldom gave your valued coins of time,
worthy things lost, not sought for,
ones years make priceless,
irretrievable.
I thought you glanced back once,
searching corners for those lost in dust.

I stroll this street as
sleepless as stars. Dawn splashes, rises,
washes the coast of all the filth of darkness past,
    casting
flakes of light on waves of gray,
painting them white
all the way to the horizon.

REMEMBER

Remember that night when water sang in the spring,
shined in the light of a moon where we abode in
a field of few words,
that night when summer stayed—
moon dressed in blue-white
one we didn't need to tilt our heads to see—
and songs of frogs along the creek
where we abode with
few words.

Remember that night when one piano
from one screened door
poured forth in the mossy mosquito night
for us.

You wrote and spoke a poem about a moon
unlike so many poems about so many moons
always broken and lonely.
Your moon was not lonely.

Remember that night when summer
felt like someone who'd come so near, so clearly blue-
    white
like the moon.

ORDER IN HAMDEN, NEW YORK

We are walking. It is evening.
The straight lane lies paved, painted
in fine white lines evenly spaced
like heart beats of time,
clock ticks of life.

We are walking. There is order.
Rows of growth growing green cover the world
like warranties in words on pages—
food for a future—these green rows cross our vision.
It is August. Blossoms promise fat roots
hidden, caked thick in red clay, potatoes waiting for
    sun.
These rows of green consume our fields of thought
    which grow so wild,
flowering unruly.

We are walking. There is order. It is evening.
We seek the wild life—fox, coyote, snake—something
    slinking out in this quiet world's order—
something sudden—just wildly alive
to take us away from us,
from our tidy disorder,
someplace secret.

It is evening. There is order.
We are walking in the wonder
full of August silence.
We look upward for the hawk's flight.
We look to look like her in her high grace, her high
    eyes.
We look to soar the august skies, but

we are walking in our order. It is evening,
and we are feeling humid air, the humiliation of
 humanness, as
we come to the poplar hollow where the stream glides
 pliant and clear.
We are searching, finding slivers of fish, silent
 transparent forms, fish—
transparent as poplar shade above us.
They sparkle, dart away
beneath this clouded glass of shallow stream
to their own secret places.
There is order. It is evening.

TUCSON SAGUARO

Stone still and old as stars,
Some resemble men,
some the cross.

In April
Blossoms burst the tops
As fluids sop the womb.

Navajos
Long ago
quenched here.

Yesterday
I paced with an axe
Through the desert.

I chose one
And swung—*grunt*!
As if the thing felt pain.

A frail trickle ran
to the arid floor,
Long held tears.

ORIOLE

You hear the call of the oriole from up atop the poplar
    tree.
Her arrival's early, moving March to May,
making us question
all our fury, all our hurry.

Her sure mate is far away;
She'll still wait for him. She'll still stay until
All of April's yellow frills fill the hillsides—
speckles over green.

BROKEN LOBSTER BUOYS

Broken free from their moorings by storm or
    lobstermen's slip,
They find them on these beaches—these buoys—
broken white spots
that dot the wide red shores
like stars the skies.

Fitting litter. Styrofoams once afloat. Traces of man's
    mess.
Light lovely irony. Those still whole with black loops
at round ends—
links to rope and trap—they take home,
scrape away seaweed mud, whitewash, dry.

Later with paint they make worlds of lighthouses,
    ships,

sails at sea, waves at wharfs, gulls at crabs,
shells and fish by cliffs and clouds; worlds
of nine mile horizons,
worlds of suns, moons, stars.

A safe escape, these worlds of curiosity
they create—free of litter, idyllic.
They could do much worse
than be painters of
broken lobster buoys.

APOSTROPHE TO TIME

Between these moon rays you hear—
A fox barking from somewhere in blots of darkness.
You sizzle across the sky in shooting stars
Audible to all.
You rise.
You fall in cycles of tides, in
Spinning circles in
Precision
Visible to all.
You wane through moons.
You fill moons
And march through months ascending heights of
    seasons.
You tick in clocks, throb in pulses, thump in hearts
Audible to all.
You are the unmasked thief of youth.
You steal years by fruitless pursuits.
We just watch you.
You're visible to all.

POET

She's too shy for the stage—child playing make
    believe, plotting, putting
Attempts at truth on white in black defiled ink.
She searches for innocence, purity's sister
Through fallen confessions, confusions, and human
    sounds.
She's the shy hider behind closed curtains of hanging
    night,
Suspending silence, prosaically waiting,
too tone deaf to sing song lyrics.

She's a child whispering wishes, a strummer of words
    and wooden stringed shouts to worlds aloud.
Pigment blind, and can't find the right shade to
    recreate creation,
Your canvas sprawls as Kansas sprawls, in tense tans,
blemished greens.
Your tones of words whisper, babble, ramble and
Shift scribbles read through dark glass.
Your words are one brush strokes sprawling glorious
    tan-green grasslands,
Soundless canvas scars searching for innocence
And still life.

THE ROAD ABOVE THE RIVERS

This road above the rivers we've often ridden.
Its bridges crossing over those moving waters,
And we hear our muffled wheels rolling and reeling
    at speeds
Exceeding ninety.

This road we've often ridden sometimes speaks to us of
Ancient paths, paths natives have trodden. It tells us old stories of cold, ice hardened,
Old paths where strong ones once walked,
Strong Native Canadians
Emerging from tall teepees, full-feathered, ready.
"Keep your moccasins on the ancient paths," they were told.
"Keep your feet where your fathers walked. Keep your feet
Where your fathers' fathers fought."

We've been down this road before.
This road we've often ridden.
She recites her poems in measure and meter and never
Finishes her long, first nation lines.

Canada stretches her arms forward
Like a tired bear
Hibernating within the doors of ice caves,
Snoring, roaring, waiting for the first cracks of spring.
These rivers slither. They're veins finding the world's heart.

These rivers slither. Pulsing as arteries, packing their bags,
Leaving the land's heart.
This road we've often ridden
Above the slithering river.

SHELTER ISLAND AUTUMN

Autumn on Shelter Island falls on small talons
Like wild birds crowded with color.
She splashes her life from her blue gulf
Smothering hastily last traces of lonesome summer.
We will wait until the last blush wanes, fades, ebbs
In the colorless dust of November.
It is over. Winter frowns, bullying his angry way,
Killing all color.

POEM FOR YOUR 58TH BIRTHDAY

Away from you today again
The view from our wide front window—I imagine
How you see our street through sheets of rain
Puddle-full at the feet of trees, how
You wake to a jay's call, and pray
For one of ours who's far from home.

I imagine you move then
to the rear of our home
you've made right and kind,
Gaze through glass—our green-gray lawn,
Search for the jay that called, and pray
For a child of ours who's far from home,

Grown now, and we remember their
Running through leaves raked high as haybales
under the slanted massive swamp maple,
stumbling through its autumn orange,
Later in winter snow—
their quiet shouts in loud white silence.

Half our lives ago our dying child—

Beautiful baby girl—her blue death impression
Locked in our worried minds—
Corpse-to-be striving for life—
so onerous to behold, so hard
to give farewells.

Away from you today again
The view from my classroom window—
High above the breadth of high tech and books—
Brings my eye on a blue jay's dart into a maple.
I pray for you as you pray
For those of ours who are far from home.

ELIJAH

One who never did die
once prayed, "Let me die."
Later a flaming chariot arrives soaring—detouring
Flying farthest—answered ancient prayer.
He prayed fervently.
The swampy world is sinking, yet
We recall the scent
Spring will bring—prevailing on the breezes
of some Sunday morning when
"The sun of righteousness shall arise with healing in
 his wings"
here in this world's swamp.

TEREBELLUM SHELL

A conch,
A little augur
Shiny-slim,

Glossy—smooth,
Pacific shell
Sand dweller
In bullet shape
With short spire
In soft pastel
Wan patterns of
Sand colors, in shape
Like the pattern on
This thin page,
A subtidal find,
finished in time,
A piece of pretty
Death to cherish
And carry away
For keeps.

MARCH SNOW

Longed for March strolls into our Canadian field.
Her sweet scent, her cold clean snow, freshly
Fallen in clear air,
In midday sun
Melts.
Her brightness blinds us. She rises above
A dozen memories
Once frozen like dreams in sleep
Remembered. She shines
in our minds, smiles with eyes
Squinting. She greets
Us, and we breathe deeply
Her warm coldness, her dripping beginnings of
    spring,

Her dozen frozen memories—old, slowly
Melting.

March meanders into our field, whitens our world.
We're in our meadow of life where
In our meadow of life the
Sure sound of the foaming sea is heard afar, is
Heard in the depth of our soul's ear.

Winter's over. March climbs
Onto our Canadian shore with life, our island's
    curves, coves, and slender creeks
That reach like fingers
Inland, searching
For earth, full with dripping beginnings of spring,
Slow midday snow-thaw, with
Old memories
Melting.

SOYBEAN FIELD

The descending
compliant rows of green from mounds of growth
Between
low shadowed corridors, shallow valleys, narrow
    gullies—
A smooth view, a raked look, a soft growth—
The wind combs the soybean field
Turning leaves to successive waves all the way up
From the bay that is down
where the pink beach thinly
Cleaves
The two —the field and sea, the green and blue—

Asunder.
And then the crows' mewling *caws* are
Cloven
By ravens' cries.
To the east the mare of the crescent moon rises
    lemon colored—
Jaundiced—a hue somewhere
Between
The spectrum's orange and green.
To the west the sun sets
In egg yolk and red,
The tide rising, gushing westward,
The wind and waves pushing eastward, and we are
Descending
On bike pedals
Down the unpaved road beside the soybean field
Against the wind—prisoners for now to this earth,
    this life—both
Earth and life, so replete with
These betweens,
These asunders,
These easts and wests,
These subtle shifts in spectrums,
These tides that rise against the driven waves,
These that fall, and all
These contraries all full of views, hues, and rides
Down hill against the wind, and
up hill with the wind.

INTRUDERS

They're dark, small,
Fallen angels some say the mad see as they
Scream in seas of confusion;
They're those that move us to cries for help.
Spring snow explodes in untimely
Thin silence, spilling thin winter—white, intruding.
The silver survivor—intruder—
Lone coyote loping over white fields,
Slowly, hungry.

We work words together in meter, build with
    syllables, prune intruders,
Puzzle musical pieces together. Words are sounds,
    sounds words,
Pieces of sense, senses of peace, voices of music
    without intruders,
Assonance recurrences, consonance recurrences.

Intruders,
The unwanted syllables,
Stunters of growth, sudden traffics, broken bones,
uncalled for callers in phones, clogs, spills, slips,
    bereavements,
Hurts in words, gestures in shoulders,
Grimace in faces, promise in frowns,
Infirmary hours, blood spills before sutures,
Blocks in roads, stops in clocks —intruders—
Steps down, leaps up.

WAKEFULNESS

The broken empty bed of this life—

Before dawn you are awake.
The mosquitoes sing songs of their longings
Clinging to summer screens
With thirst for blood.

August darkness on Panmure Island hills—

The sky's bereft of stars; the moon's in bloom,
Blurred in vapors over the oval field.
An array of potato blossoms blazes.

Below your window—so close—
One cricket speaks.
From here you hear a lone coyote's cry
Far across salt marsh, farther across the bay—

His high pitch stretching westward
Piercing pre-dawn distance through silence
With thrusts of thirsting loneliness,
Reaching—I suppose—your soul only.

Wakefulness fills these rooms like squally wind.
Dawn begins to lighten this visible world,
permitting a quilt of mist, unruffled
To rest upon the land and sea, before
the empty broken bed of this world.

BLUEFISH

Sea swells endure in glossed forest green.
The sky lies glazed in gray.
Fine rain falls, spraying mist mixed with salt.

Fresh red speckles splash clots
In drops of bluefish blood, soaking the white
shining deck.

Bloody shoe prints smear—
Evidence in dances of violence.
They've fallen, all of them—

Fish buckets full—
To our deceitful lures,
Lost their sea-free lives

To devilish hooks, lines, sinkers,
Hungry human hands, knives, plates...
The struggle, the catch—

They rise above a surface of sea,
Ascend into death. Slimy tails slap.
Gills grapple for breath,

This ancient world
Continues its spinning, whirling
Imperfect balance—

Peculiar,
As on the spinning wheel
In the pottery barn.

A NEW APOSTROPHE TO TIME

You're the grinless sheriff
Handcuffing my days
Into limitations.
Your prison cell
Like a shoreline:
Here and no farther,
Now and no further.

SAINTS

They descend into sleep,
The dream realm of valleys, dry streams
Filled with dry bones.

Fantasies rise as a phoenix
In white resurrection
From ashes,

In swirls of stars,
Swelling waters,
And foreign countries.

They awaken.
They brush off the dust
Of paltry death.

MILE FAR BONFIRE

We see this bright glow, hear its commotion—
intensity of light, singleness of sound.

A mile-far bonfire across a sprawling Illinois hill
From here a mere candle
Dulled and quelled by distance and darkness—
a mere murmur of burning through winter silence
In lulled muffled laughs—fire's noises, quiet voices—
A hallowed unity, a holy union—
Flaming laser radiance
Set apart
From cold.

Mile-far sparks fly upward into stars
The sure way starling clusters soar into wind.
Golden flakes of fire rise sending embers ascending

mixing in the Milky Way's hazed
Eternal soft fog, blend of blue-light wonder.

Beyond the fire the horizon lies east to west.
Trunks' and limbs' winter silhouettes
Hibernate in dormancy, stone frozen
Hiding in sleep, death's similitude,
Hidden, aglow by firelight—
promise of resurrection, ascension,
Light, life.

A TIME TO THROW AWAY

Search memory,
Rummage under rubble
In moth-balled cellar
Of yellowed past.
Dig out debris, dross,
Worthless odds, ends
Fit for the trash heap.
Toss them there to fester
In fires of burning forgetfulness
Forever.

Search memory
Carefully slide out,
Wash, polish, shine
Those items of returned desire.
Find the worthwhile pieces
For the window show—out, festive—
Show to those who remember tomorrow
The final fires of His refining
The crucible for silver.

WATERFALLS

Rain cascades, slides to waterfalls.
Slivers of silver streams tinted sallow by a setting sun
Stumble down slipping
Sliding headlong
Into the long oval lake which loves
To swallow—chin lifted, head tilted
drinking—
all the water
Falling.

THE SOUND OF WIND

When you last loved the sound of wind moving
    through trees—
God impelled—
Swiveling, whistling, whirling
Into the high limbs of winter,
Or strumming the willowy limbs of summer,
You were young.

Now you just listen to the fine-tuned gusts and
Wonder ,
What is it it utters to us, this wind?
The stronger the force the more mellifluous the lilt—
    music that lifts
like choruses, crescendos ascending in breakings of
    branches,
Then pauses, falters, softens.

When you last loved the sound of wind moving
    through trees—
God impelled—

Sent and loosened like light
Over water moving, roaring in whispers of winter,
Or whispering roars in summer,
You were young.

Now you just listen—
Invisible hands of wind caressing the surface of sea,
    and
Wonder what is it it intones to us, this wind?
The swell of a wave rises in silence,
Then falls, falters, crashing in breaking crescendo,
Like the breaking of branches, the toppling of trunks,
The brokenness of youth.

FLEEING MOUSE

Fleeing mouse across the freeway leaps,
Dashing safely into sky-scraping weeds,
Then dances—we imagine—an
Innocent dance—puerile joy, having escaped
Unscathed—
As we prowl over, passing
On four power driven wheels
Speeding through Salina, Kansas.

SNAKES

Snakes lurk, bark with snarls of rotwilers
Pitbulls, and wolves.
We speak your name, Jesus.
They turn—
tails between legs—
Lost, powerless
defeated hisses.

BROWN TROUT, WOODSTOCK, NEW HAMPSHIRE

Brown trout glide with power, fly through water currents.
Sparrows swim through heavy air, and here we are
Seated beside this quiet
               Winding
Waterway,
Leaning, looking,
trying to see as trout would, or sparrows could,
held by chains of human weakness,
held by humanness.

SIX INNINGS

In our over-the-hill fifties
We drive west in the pick-up—
Radio baseball spoken motion through speakers—
Midday summer sounds are whispers.
Air whirls in the small world of the cab—
Wind through open windows.
We've finished six innings—
This pastime we call life.

Cumulus clouds like mountains mushroom upward.
They fill the sky in the south—mounds of pillowy white—
Shadow colors, shades of coal-gray.
The open road sends reminiscences—
Yearnings for yesterdays, tomorrow's longing—
The sun breaks, sends its streaks,
visible flashes of moving light.

Invisible wind—the treasures of heaven
Blow through hidden straws of angels, billowing
Over yellow fields of winter wheat.

We've finished six innings—
This pastime, this game.

HURRICANE SANDY

While all spun above us
Houses cartwheeled under a moon
Hidden by clouds smacked about with God's scythe.
We heard the sound of many waters,
Wondered what the fish felt under a serene crust of sea,
Remembering the fixed galaxy emblazoned
Across blackened spirals of the universe
While all spun in chaos just above us.

SUMMER FIELD

There's something sorrowful about the summer field.
His face sits in ignominy,
a shame of isolation
By the Prince Edward Island bayside.
Walk to the corner where the tractor turned a lazy turn,
Where the brush hog missed some young sprung saplings.
It's there—in the place of painful snubs and rebuffs
we hear a voice speaking with sureness
surpassing the suffering of slights.

GREEN HOUSES

Emerald buildings,
Transparent iridescence,
Shells in symmetry—
God's vision through and
into thin human skins,
Symmetrical order—immortal
life residing within.
Limpid transparency
Pulsating greenness
Of life rising from wet, hot loam
All glowing through.

HEAVEN'S DIMENSIONS

The mulberry tree bleeds
All over white pavement.
Heaven's heavy dimensions are mentioned—
Turn the page and see.

Elms potently plunge upward
Like fountains of living water.
Jesus, at your feet we sit—
Sixty years.

GRAND DAD

Smoker of Lucky Strikes, loud laugher,
Man who used pliers to pull rotting teeth—
I still recall those ruddy blood clots spat
At the chipped, white, porcelain sink.
You didn't even bend your torso.
Old soldier, trooper with wounds,

Broken Prose, Spoken Poems

You taught me—little kid—
to eat my peas without gagging.
"Mix 'em in the mashed potatoes!
Pepper! Pepper!"
You taught tough tenderness,
lived tender toughness.
Your broken poetic prose,
in my memory spoken
From a heart as vibrant
As Brooklyn, as big as New York.
From that toothless mouth you shouted
Into my little affected ears—
sardonically sensitively
Under the loud mouthed shadows
Of screaming jets descending to Kennedy:
"Don't be ashamed to cry! I'm not ashamed to cry!"
And you did just that, once glazing your face with tears,
"Some things make me cry!" you said with your New York lilt.
You cried when the Yankees won—watching grown men
Who'd triumphed in child's play—the leaping team like children
When the World Series was won up in the Bronx.

EVANGELIST

Fiery old preacher full of amplified fury,
Over-boldness blazing over the railroad yard.
Tall, tilted tent.
Plum pulpit
Flimsy in the field—that field that years earlier
Had grown something yielding, willowy, yellow—

Maybe barley, possibly wheat.

Old bard of coatless poems come in summer from afar—
somewhere in Canada, land of Midwest widths, to our small county's
Corner—come with loud life, flaming fists,
index fingers staring
Down
Our stony smoky souls, our adolescents drunk in beer,
Adults in secret sins, smoldering.

Here you hatch—bizarre bird chirping words, catching
Ears, eyes, us by surprise, evangelize
In flames of loving rage.
God. That angry? We wondered, squinting at sunset.
When the sermon's story closes,
Your homeless poem folds—you weep, weep, weep
feeling God's melted heart of fire.

SOMEHOW OUT HERE

Somehow out here on the lake shore
He makes us breakfast: baked bread,

Broken Prose, Spoken Poems 51

Broiled fish—foot long rainbows—cleaned,
Seasoned with salt, basil, and bayleaves,
lemon basted,
Cooked over olive wood coals.
A dry swept morning.

Somehow out here from this little ship
Where we've drifted from our mooring, moonless and
Mourning, delirious and starless, weary
With rocking in labor and waves—nets filled
With emptiness—
He blends in in this yellow sun-soaked dawn unrecognized,
Far on the steady shore.

Somehow out here we know
Who this is in this familiar distance standing,
And we're drawn, dragging a sudden harvest, garnered,
Too heavy to haul to shore.
One plunges in in sudden swim ecstatic toward
The sure golden shore. Ours are faces of children
shining in tears before father.

How can we ever say,
"We're sorry" with all that we recall?
His steady gaze,
His cadent tone
Somehow out here
In the sallow washed-out dawn
Tells us He's forgotten.

WAKING FROM A DREAM

Within a dry July night
Our clock ticks its black rhythm.
Skunks poke noses through thick clover searching for
    grubs.
We rise from sleep as shallow as eyelids, dreaming of
Our dying father.

He is young, in this dream, chasing us in earnest
    seeking, calling—
His voice, our names.
We're running from him—a convolution of hallways,
doorways,
alleyway mazes,
weaving
Through our childhood parish—all a fallen,
broken confusion.

For decades We've been hiding
Behind walls of words, joke making,
shielded smiles, cordial laughs, gates of silence,
    knowing
From ancient scripture—
Wisdom whispers blends of truth with love.

We arrive here
To these hours, Dad's death, evening,
A hallway light—
Fresh wrinkles in midnight's mirror—
Old foresworn sins elbowing our ribs.
Garrulous guilt grows, yet we know of the irony
in God's great blood that bathes, makes
White as wool and snow.

Flip a switch on the back porch.
A flood lamp chases darkness and skunks—
Their black bobbing across gradual darkening, across
Grassy clover and black-green.

God, between us—us and you—
A stench of skunk,
The soft moss grown sound of surfacing rain, a sky of
 dark glass,
One open hole where a cluster of stars sparkles like
 ice—
Our cries ascending through.

SEA SIDE

Our pace changes on a day by the sea side—
Umbrella colors in yellow air
Follow cloud shadows
Shoving blue aside with
Rude shoulders.
Clouds move over,
build room for sun, then
Crowd him out again.
Frisbees fly freely. Kites fly tied.
Flamboyant balls flurry above
Sprawling water—lucid, white, strident—
Below outspoken floating gulls.
One long brush stroke of human voices blended with
 waves,
The rising tide, the falling tide,
The sun's striding across the steadfast sky,
Youthful white clouds dodging time.

WAITING

Can't help but scribble little words while she waits for
   You God,
Can't help but write words this night, words while
   she waits for You.
She can't help but speak to You from these fields of
   words
Of weeds she wants pulled
from the soil of her heart.
It's Your words she gulps down—
those fixed in stars, always filling the vacant places
   out there
Within her.

BRIDGES

One stretches long across the sprawling width of
   water, nine miles
Conquering the width of Northumberland Strait,
Connecting whole Provinces: New Brunswick and
   Prince Edward Island—
Structure strengthened in mortar, human
   construction stretching
Engineered in girders and pilings conducting people
   who've purposes.

Another's
Small boards
Fastening
two forests,
Making one,
Crossing thin stream—
Black slither of

Water winding,
Splitting a forest
in two in pink
dawn darkness
over winter snow
languished in blue.
Bridges—

Connecting rods sending power,
Ancient aqueducts conducting water,
Red threads tying two
broken worlds.

The bridge-trestle traversing Long Island Railroad trains
Over Montauk Highway in Sometown, New York
Broke last year—severed—broken infrastructure,
Divorced, cutting the marriage of two townships.
Nothing to do but rebuild, strengthen, consume time, reconnect.

WINTER HOURS

Fisted hands have held handles of axes.
Sinews have swung their heads
Down,
have lifted, split, and stacked
up in Canada.
We've counted the hours of winter,
Measured the nerves of trembling survival,
wondering on our wanderings
Between walls,
Worn, wearing shadows cast by deep true light.

ALL AFTERNOON

Mauve southbound clouds move through blue
    heavens
All afternoon long. Their flickering shadows
Fall face down on the Ontario
Hay field—ghosts of decades gone.

That same wind as through these spruces whispers,
    pushes.
Evergreen boughs are sprung from trunks,
Trunks sprung from roots anchored—
Networks meshed, woven, rooted in sour ground.

These boughs, as arms
Bow,
waving farewell to clouds and shadows
All sunlight long.

MAINE CHAIN LINK

The creator's fingers set far away and neatly
The lake where it lay for our full view—
A puddle between three mountains—
Rain and gravity's rendezvous,
Fastened sheet of fragile glass,
Still waters holding frantic life

Hidden underneath, unseen
In dim depths of green.
It's where the lake trout fans fins,
And flurries his sturdy tail
In round turns and with no thought
In soundless swarms of slow circles

Intent in instinct, in hungry creature searches.
We wend our way down the winding
Sloping path pacing
Making space from our place in these hills,
Rods and reels in ready hands—
Intent in instinct, hungry savages searching.

PASTURE

In the west the sentinel Venus sits. He is alert.
Tired old crescent moon reclines, leans back on his rocker
Reading in the den of dusk's east. Down here
Windy beeches and windy birches bow at the field's edge.
In the middle, one lone elm lifts limbs heavenward—maestro
Leading the trivial trees—giving homage in symphony.

The playful calf—she comes to me
Like a grandchild with nerve
Wearing little grin—I imagine—and
Little skip. This day—sweltered
With counting and human labor—
I almost forget how to play.

TIME TO PRUNE

Promises, a month of Mondays—
Moon phases—some nights never seen, just
images imagined, predictable shapes—
Those phases—hidden as we hear rain and
Clouds winged by wind.

One waning gibbous Monday the gardener pruned.
We found a little tree standing handsomely. Look!
It appeared; never noticed. Then time
Permitted vines to climb, overwhelm,
Drown its life under.

Removals of strongholds, choke, foot, and other holds,
Grips of grim death—those severe severings
In our lives—hurtful prunings
Helping us love God in death of self—
Even in pain.

AMERICAN KESTREL

Neighborhood bully,
Bird of prey shoulders his way—
Loud killer of small birds and mice,
Falcon mimicry,
High perched perimeter watcher,
Dalliance diver, searching,
Screeching in flight
On Panmure Island.

Demanding notice at the air show
Four came to our field for summer.
The hummingbird feeder full of nectar—
The hummingbird fears keep them far.
They hear the kestrels
from dark forest shadows.
They hide from mean kestrels,
Those neighborhood bullies.

FLASHES OF MEMORY

We revisit with inner eyes memory flashes
All in sunlight, all in color—green and blue.
We hear the harps of years in the far heart of song,
Softly sung in our ears.

They smell the scents of summer sent from the sea,
feel fingers feeling fingers, and
taste the taste of fowl and fish
At tables firmly fit—

Decades into the well lit rooms
of memory—
Green eyes gazing into blue,
blue into green.

Children, labor, sleep, sighs, sips, cries,
Senior citizenship, storms, films, photos,
Phone calls and phone calls unreturned, unheard—
Even eighty years—

A flash, a year, a day that vanishes as a vapor
That seems to never end, but ends a vapor
all for something
"eternal in the heavens."

FIRST BORN

I've favorite unforgotten remembrances—
Your birthday, for one, as vivid
As an hour ago, holding you in your first mantle,
Speaking meekly, repeating your name.
Your cries subside, finding
Your breath, more breaths,

giving one little infant grin.
Other unforgotten remembrances—
Your beaming birthday face
and Christmas cracks of dawn...
And those drives, just us, long talks
To college, once lost by New Bedford,
But feeling fine if the drive took days.
Time with you, rest from life.
I remember your wedding day,
Your beaming wedding face.
I've favorite unforgotten recollections
Collected in thirty-four years.

BLUE BROKEN MUSSEL SHELLS

They shine on the wet shoreline—
Blue fool's gold for sea glass seekers
Who search for the piece of great price—
The blue, amber, red piece of sea glass—
The shard of farther history,
The painful traces, slivers of another time,
Wound makers healed smooth, softened by sea,
Fully colorful. You can spot them,
the sea glass seekers, that is.

They slowly stroll in bare feet, heads bowed
Crouching searchers. Bend, reach, lift, look—
They learn they've been lured by a beach devil's
    deceit,
Crustacean skeletons—
Blue broken mussel shells—
From the ripples of man's first fallen brokenness,

When he was sought for by Him who valued him who
    was lost in
Flimsy death, the remains.

The strong fingers of storms and tides comb, comb,
And comb again, raising old sea glass from beneath
    time's sand—
The weighty stones sink and frivolous
sea glass rises, repeats rising, to their shapely colors,
The pellucid to pearly white.

Transparent lusters appear
Above the crystals of quartz, gravel, and stone—
Gifts from the past, the human past.
Fingers excavate, sort, search. Nothing resurrects
    them like
The combing of the sea—the tide,
The storm, combed through smooth—
Soft shards of thousands of yesterdays,
Even a hundred years—
shards separated from shells—
Preserved ruins of the labors of man,
Old ocean worn, sea broken glass.

OPERATING ROOM

We wheeled you into that well lit whitened room
Where blue mask faces waited in blue aura
And Bronx darkness
Washed and scrubbed.
Hands held eye level scalpels.
We backed away wildly afraid, unable to gape.
We prayed through the long night
Far far from the sight.

NUMBER SIX DREAMS

Number six sticks on my old jersey—gold over
    purple—
That dream recurs in color
In green fields, yellow goals in white frames,
yellow cards in handballs, near scores
that never splatter the back of the net.

Number six dreams—
Broken dreams, broken hope,
Muddy slumps in autumn losses,
Fast passes, long crosses, headers, traps, tackles,
Lone walks to buses, limps to lockers, hobbles to
    showers,
Lumps, bumps, hidden whimpers.

Dreams, wearing number six, where
Goalkeeper's saves made in dreams in fields of
    sleep—
Dreams where you never get there, can't finish,
Never reach your search—*thumps* of balls on far
    posts—
Almosts. Goals always only almost.

Dreams, wearing number six,
Dreams in drab disappointment,
Obstructive foilings, hindered, impeded—
Heavy rains on game days—lose by one—
The spotted ball, round dice flying, opposed, blocked,
    closed—
another almost—

number six, one shy,
only almost.

BROKEN POEM

The
Broken poem
That lolls in free verse excuse
For broken rhyme scheme,
Broken meter and all the word order patterns
That make our world orderly
Is just simply broken, unfinished, always
Saved to work on on a later day
When there's time or eternity to make
Unbroken, fixed, finished in redemption.

The
Broken stuff—
Are they still stuff? A
Broken bike is still a bike.
Broken heart, dream, promise—
a heart, a dream, a promise still.
We walked through gardens on broken slate,
On walks of broken boards, sturdy
With strong legs and good boots,
And we're broken.

The
Broken humans
Hurt, unhealed, harrowed, plowed
Before the seed is planted, or water poured—
Asleep in deep sleep on broken beds
Snoring, dreaming broken dreams.
Broken beings broken by beings who are also
Broken—some by unseen demons—
souls afloat in a world that is broken,
Fallen, stolen, waiting for redemption.

SPOKEN PROSE

I

Teach us to pray.
We seem to learn best about praying when placed in
Arduous places,
Hopeless places—places that remain hopeless
 without Him—
Places only He undertakes ably,
places calling for prayer—these places
Teach us to pray.

We are fallen creatures.
We can't rise without our creator, without praying,
calling His grace, forgiveness… Him.
We're stuck under slimy stones
Away from our Creator.
We are fallen creatures.
The Lord's model is the cornerstone,

The great foundation to build upon:
"Give us this day our daily bread":
The great synecdoche for all we need—sustenance to
 live—
"Give us all we need to do your will!
Give us that bread."
The Lord's model is the cornerstone.

"Forgive us our trespasses
As we forgive those who trespass against us."
The river's frozen without forgiveness.
Forgive! There's no survival in living short of
 forgiving crimes,

No movement, no horizontal health, no vertical
> breath.
We forgive.
"Forgive us our trespasses."

"Thy will be done."
A far goal line, a massive waiver.
Praying is getting in God's line, placed in our places
Underneath His gentle gavel. Praying is not pushing,
Squeezing, jamming
Into our corner, our maker,
underneath our will.
"Thy will be done."

II

"Be anxious for nothing,
but in everything by prayer and supplication,
with thanksgiving,
let your requests be made known to God;
and the peace of God,
which surpasses all understanding
will guard your hearts and minds through Christ
> Jesus." Philippians 4:6,7

Paul the Apostle's pen to friends:
"We wanted to come to you—even I, Paul—time and
> time again, but Satan hindered us." —the sole
> scripture—the sabotage of Paul's good plans—
not imputed to God's direct barrier.
Other barricades fold him under the Holy Spirit's
> forbiddance—
To go here, to preach there.

"Lest I be exalted above measure (by the many
　　revelations of heaven)
A thorn of the flesh was given to me...
Three times
I pleaded...cried...requested..."
God's return? "My grace is enough...
My strength is made perfect through weakness."
Lowering, for those who pray,
When we or ours are broken.

Our Father permits our enemy to punch, thump, cuff
　　us—
Our enemy bound to Father's will,
ignorant of his undesigned strengthening of
The Father's children.
Nothing afflicts
Beyond our Father's nod—His
Permission granted. Our prayer persists:
Thy will be done. Hinder our will.

III

In Israel's history, "They lusted greatly in the desert,
And tested God, and He gave them their request,
But sent leanness into their soul." *Psalm 106:13,14*
A steep price to pay—
When we pray, Our will be done.

God authors disappointments,
Pens our difficult stories,
Molds our painful quarantines,
Forges our links of chain,
Piles upward the mountains we climb.
He carries us over His higher purposes:

Our journey, the light at our feet—
His likeness. Our destination.

"I know the plans I have for you…a future…a hope."
Jeremiah 29:11
He gives what's noble: a thorn, a thwarted plan;
And it's there we learn He meets our need, gives our daily bread.
"Whatever the Lord pleases He does." *Psalm 35:6*
I do what I will, but still
I want your prayer, part of my plan.
Trust me with all your heart.
"Lean not on your own understanding."
Acknowledge Me in all your ways.
I'll direct your paths.

IV

God answers Job's questions with questions.
His broken world broken apart: kids, health, wealth killed.
He pleads, receiving peace that transcends understanding.
God's queries answer queries. Job surrenders,
"I spoke of things I don't understand, too wonderful for me." *Job 42:3*.
Job gets it. We get it. What?
The idea that we don't get it.
Your will be done. Your ways are higher.
You know what you're doing. You do what You will.
You want us on board. You rest in the boat, at peace in the storm.
We're going to the other side.
You said so.

V

Jesus prays, in skirmish with His humanness,
to His Father at the edge of the end.
"Let this cup pass from me. Nevertheless, not My will, but Yours
Be done." Staring down the cross,
He prays, entreats His Father, knowing
His limit without Him.
He never knew the day or hour of His return,
Never knew who'd sit with Him
In His kingdom.
He learned obedience through His suffering.
He learned dependence on His Father.
Lived in the power of submission, the Father's will.
Not until His triumph over death He proclaims,
"All authority and power in heaven and on earth has been given to me."
And He gives to us, as we yield to Him, to do His will.
Face to face with Pilate, "You would have no power over Me unless
It were given to you from the Father above."

THE PAST

Memory, the past.
The sound in a scent, the touch of a sight,
Something subtle touching some sense—
A taste in time suddenly brings me there—
Down
Dragged to those
sunken stones
At the bottom of the sea
Where vivid words are chiseled, still images.

Memory. The past.
Just a song, or a scent,
Something soft touching some sense—
Four chords suddenly brings them here,
clear, up from depths with sounds of stringed
    instruments
Pumped up with air to breathing surfaces, clear,
Then higher in air farther to clear heavens—
Hot air balloons bursting,
Rising full with color.

Memory. The past.
We search pages for an old page of pain,
The weighty warm ache of memory,
A photograph, an old stone,
An unforgotten gist,
an ache of pleasure.

CONDITIONAL LOVE

The consummate oxymoron—
The conditional love fastened to hate—
Heated and basted in hatred—
It's the painted face, the hidden rust,
Termites unseen in the cellar ceiling.

You said you'd come back to me if….
And then there was silence,
The hatred of cold conditions,
The lostness of loose promises,
The slammed door, the self's demands
The bolted lock, the lies,
The tantrum.

What more could He relinquish?
the donor with no conditions?
With thorny coronet, bloodied beardless face,
Carrying curses, lashes, betrayal,
Slanders, dishonor, and worse
with a cross?

SOD FARM MEDITATION

Kelly green leaves of grass by the trillions
make velvet carpet verdant for acres
As far as eyes see.

Tires of tractors roll.
Forks of hi-lows load.
Beds of trailers haul.

Grow them here; move them there.
We walk in a world that shifts and swirls.
We crawl on earth that quakes.

Anchors stay; transplants change.
The floor of ages shifts.
Leaves and mortals come and go,

Enter, exit.
Kept vows keep promising.
Betrayals stay extant.

To and fro, fast we go,
Bearing bags of seed, carting tears in flasks
To scatter here, broadcast there.

Shallow roots suffer
unheard
Until our welcome home.

SITTING

Sitting. Just sitting.
Sit still! Stay put!
Days pass. Weeks, months...
Still sitting, waiting through
Days. Be still. Learn to be still.

Study in sitting, in stillness.
Just sit still in the mystery of stillness,
In the cushion of fallen quills of running time.
Wait. Wait in the court room
Of the planet. Sit. Wait.

A lark sits on the gutter guard,
With creased wings folded closed.
Time descends its vertical slide
With paws of patient speed
And legs of swift patience.

The sun rose in tints of rose
And fell in hues of yellow.
Her face smiled; her mien frowned.
A lark sings on the gutter guard,
With creased wings folded closed.

EASTERN NEW MEXICO

Eastern New Mexico, replete with emptiness;
Like sprawling parchment postponed for words,
A vast canvas waiting for paint—
Purposeless spaces of austere expanse,
Parched width, scope of sky
And hues
Lies before us,

so business-like
with bulges, bumps like warts on skin.
The open road bursts ahead, splurging
Westward into sprawling vastness—New Mexico—
Onward toward the frowning smiles of our futures,
Forward toward a scrubbed flat morrow,
Like sprawling parchment postponed for words—
The secretive likelihoods of our lives

SILHOUETTES AT SUNSET

Sunset seethes in the western sky—
fire aflame in sleek ribbons streaking across space,
Tangerine tinge.
Silhouettes of evergreens on the periphery of hills,
of limbs and drizzles of twigs
lingering through placid black shadow-lands
where we sojourn.

We listen all life long
To tunes of silver-tongued fowl—
The watchman owl, lovesick nightingale—
All nightfall long.
Forever in seminary, it seems,
Always learning to—"count"
through diverse trials,
in refining fires—"it all joy" probing
For gold in glaring glory
Somewhere at the end of the open road.

Dawn rises above hours of sleep
to her feet, and
We'll rise to ours, stride as
roaming pilgrims

holding closely the trail guide's rope, lifting
Fellow visitors who faint along the way
wearing shoes that never wear,
Ever sure to get there.

A VAPOR

I hear a human voice, lyrics, Neil Young
harmonica, piano, strings in song.
They all thrust me back thirty-three years.

"What is your life?"

I smell the smell from a pan frying fish.
I'm back farther, grandma's kitchen.
I'm seven again.

"It is only a vapor."

I see a pretty Chevy 63' pickup, blue,
parked on Parkside.
Swiftly my mind revisits its time.

"It appears for a little while and then vanishes"

Whoosshh! What was that?
flashbacks of places gone, your life my friend.
Can I do that over?

"away."

Honks of geese soar overhead, pass out of sight
Southward like gentle jets,
Never to be seen, heard, felt again.

INDIANAPOLIS

Interstate lit by high
lights snakes around
limits of Indianapolis
where human race lives—
mystery city, modern
ghost town of the
impious late hour—
semi-skyscraping
downtown in space
age aura—blue neon
rectangular crowns,
structures aglow
in light blinking
summer haze like
rocket ships within
the final countdown.

Long spinning hours of darkness recline behind our tired tires
As far as Columbus, Ohio; even farther east.
Pleasing welcomed lights of Indianapolis ignite
this small corner of the measureless Midwestern night
daubing darkness's fourth watch in lofty mauve-blue.
Beneath the starry depths of the universe this infinitesimal city—
This Indianapolis—reposes like a spark, a small waning campfire—
The last embers aglow in one small campsite in the immeasurable cosmos.

SNOWFALL AND WOOL

Sin's strewn like satellites of cancer—sickly reddish
Gnawing all surrounding cells,
Strewn like crimson debris shivering
In cold, frozen interstellar space
Across exposed expanse,
The galactic barrier of planetary void.

It spreads itself scattered
Littering a scope of cityscape—
An ugly dispersion of filth
In scarlet lots of scraps: old tires, broken fixtures, broken
Blocks, rusted bikes, cracked plastics, worthless drivel, wasted
Gibberish, rubbish, junk, just brokenness.

"Let us reason..." a voice of grace.
A woolen mantle in warm white layers slides
Down, descending, covering the reaches of red
dark universe—congenial, relieving. Snow drifts down in thickness,
in soft widths of whiteness—snowfall
covering, smothering ugly sin.

STOVE FIRE

Indoors in the stove we build fire
Where roaring sounds grow loud like wind,
Flames blaze, thick strips of locust bark sizzle,
Kindle, snap sparks up from sun red embers.
From trunks of old oaks we drop chunks
Like bulky stones,

Down deep
Into the breathing, coughing chest—
this cast iron stove.

Smoke blows through, up the flue from the smokestack
Fogging sky, hiding stars.
A restful sound sounds a distant singing in the slow hours of burning
Where white wood reduces
to ashen ashes
in blue flames
waving, fanning upward, whistling,
Snapping muffled—pronouncing words
we've never learned.

REBUILD

One year beavers conspired to build their lodge
At a dipping bend in the Sturgeon River.
They labored with and without patience—
arm in arm with the steady obstinacy of time.

Their dam did what dams do, jamming the flow,
shifting the river's route. These mammals felt well
In their modern dam, but flooded
A riverfront human home.

The humans became compelled to rebuild,
Raise their foundation
Arm in arm with the steady obstinacy of time, until
They were pleased, beavers pleased, river pleased.

Years passed. Great rains came on the lax back
Of three feet of snow. Water like wet earth surged

Crumbling the dam. The river found its former
> course.
The beavers, compelled to rebuild, began.

THE PARDONER

He wanted to be the executioner, one
Who ties the knot, hanging hoods over shamefaced
> faces,
Or one who opens the gallows'
Trap door
Dropping the culpable
Only so far—before the floor.
He wanted to be the executioner, one
releasing volts, gas, guillotine blades, one
lighting the fire, one
driving the nails.
He wanted... until he dreamed he saw himself—
Mirrored stare as he swung from the rope,
Nailed, wired, ported, peering into the bottom
Of the French basket,
Beneath the guillotine praying,
Guilty.

He wants to be the pardoner, the carrier of keys
Unlocking gated locks,
Following orders of a justice—righteous,
Who sets the captive, guilty,
remorseful free.

GALVANIZED BUCKET

My galvanized bucket

Lasted long—Decades.
She hardly rusted, remained hard,
A hard to crack
Or puncture vessel.
That pail held water,
Kept the heat of shoveled embers
From burning our world down.

Somehow
in her old age she
faltered onto the thruway of
the driveway,
Compressed, perishing
In sardonic sudden death.

She's planted in the garden
Full of soft soil, with
Tulips, hyacinth,
And daffodil bulbs—
Memorial for
A faithful servant.

FISHERS ISLAND FERRY VIEW

The sky's an upside down sea:
Low curling clouds cling to cold slow winds,

Crumpled stratus clouds resist, remain fixed, above.
The ferry rocks. We remember

we watched you walk toward your truck
Over the lot's black blankness,

Alone, unlike
These couplets—

Alone, like this lone line—

Diagonally freely across the fused
White-lined well-ordered open-ended squares

Painted straight and tidy for cars'
Parking order, so like those confining

"Fill your name in the empty spaces provided"
Guidelines for the applications:

Tomorrow's hopes, impending prospects,
Possible promises.

SON

When you were a child—
small, scared, tired—
You clung, crying, "Piggy back Daddy!"
We'd play—little knuckles against my throat, legs
    draped;
Or seated on shoulders, high, so close.

And when in deep snow I stepped short steps
So you could follow, pintsized legs fell in like posts:
"It's easy when I go in your shoe-holes Dad!"
You'd raise high knees, find foreseen prints,
learn to unburden your walk with your Father.

"Follow me as I follow Father,"
Was the chant; then you grew to that interval when
individualism found independence,
until, at best you followed at a distance;
at worst, got lost.

GREAT HORNED OWL

A still sun peers into cold dark depth of woods,
Into reeds down trails that swerve
And coil
along the river, wandering
Into marshes along the bay.

Midday tide slides low and sun peaks high,
shining, spreading gold over silver shoals,
over a gray surface of the inlet from the bay.
The laurel leaves curl in the cold bred by the solstice.
Up the sandy trail the constant calls of crows cluster
    in the high limbs
Within the shelter of winter trees,
Where one wide great horned owl launches
From low perch on silent wings—alone, away
From badgering black crows, evading
Trunks of trees in
low, silent flight, maneuvering
swift colossal grace
like a slithering snake,
Escaping.

Exquisite sacred bird—
Weary, wearing scared confidence in suave posture
Wearing strange hate in sinister eyes as old as a
    devil's, head
Melded in bloated shoulders,
swiveling,
watching with feline eyes,
Hissing, hiding fear in the guise of wide shoulders,
lifting the thick weight of darkness in the forest.
She clicked her bill in the winter stillness.

Broken Prose, Spoken Poems

Was it some stolen carrion that made the black
    scavengers furious?
Something this hunter killed that had them
    uproarious?
Was it sleep these crows from this owl stole?
What rendered this stalker so helpless?
What made this darkness dweller bewildered in
    light?
What made this victor of night a victim of rickety
    birds of day?

In gold-gray glare of solstice light,
The great owl fled from limb to limb shrieking in
    weakness.
The winter had bitten in, ice gripped as the sun
descended in fields like flocks,
In woods and freezing inlets of creeks and bay
Where deciduous trees freeze,
And long brown grass lay matted
under thin broken icing of snow.

Trunks, limbs, twigs of oaks become scribbles in
    black
Against yellow glow of the fiery fall of day.

This wilderness
Like the human race is
crowded gardens of darkness.
Tree trunks are torsos, limbs arms, twigs fingers,
So many hands reaching for light.

The icy sky grows far and clear. Stars poise
Nearer than a crescent moon
Hanging within the limbs,

Swinging as a pendulum, waning.
Constellations dance as though on a stage of the
 earth's edge
Across the falling distance in fields of darkening
 skies.

SNATCHED

Six of you as babes we snatched
From dirty rooms and smoky streets
Of Addis Ababa and Brooklyn,
Seoul and South Bronx
Where birth mothers birthed you.
We washed you with water and love
Beside the watercourse among
Water lilies, watering you with
Firmness and blemished nurture.
We limped along in broken limbed
Imbalance, shortfalls in coffers,
Weariness and sickness,
Blue-collar toil in grueling hours.
Now we find you in front of facebook,
Screen games, and phone screens,
In university halls, soccer, baseball
And other fields; changing your
Offspring's diapers and tantrums,
Following your own unruly rules,
forgetting scripture verses
We ordered, rewarded you to learn.
We pointed and pushed
You in the route we ourselves
Had somehow by fluke luck,

divine providence—blindfolded
Found in our youthful lostness—
In the shadow of the cross of
Our high hero, Jesus Christ—
Having been lost in a lost world
Ourselves—but snatched ourselves
From dirty rooms and smoky streets,
Placed in the safe place of honest
flawless promises.

REJECTION

It shades in hoary grays—
Shadows in ashen gloom, overcast
As in the unreturned "Hello."

You're unfit for the shelf,
Not worth the work, rework,
Any renovation, reconciliation;

Unfit for the attic,
Amiss, out of tune, missing strings, keys,
You're remiss refuse.

Distressing message
Found in a bottle afloat,
"We're sorry but... we regret to inform you..."

The college, position, proposal,
divorce, denial, door slam,
Unanswered mail—

It shades in hoary grays—
Shadows in ashen gloom, overcast:
As in the returned "I don't want you."

POETRY

This careful language laced in grace,
Antiphonal tongues in lines in lyrical tones, in cadence-sense,
in sentences—

What is it it recites to us
spelled in blood-ink spilled into printers?

Orderly violence lancing language,
Order drawn from order,
Sought out in babel, ravel, fog—
Pattern in sense's sound and sound's sense—
highest antithesis, supreme antipathy—
Shards of words like broken jars in the potter's
    shop—
reassembled, discarded, renewed in
hands on clay at the wheel, watered with tears
Healing, spinning fresh vessels
And vowels.

This laced language—what is it it leaves us?
Like water waiting lukewarm in
Sounds in the cellar heater reshaping cold to hot;
renovation of plain prose purposed toward perfect
    verse,
always a *nearly*, only an *almost*—
The dragged net of fish to shore,
their flapping life in dying.

This careful language—what is it it sings to us?
the finer part fitted for the finer site,
The tuning in the keys,
Restoration of a broken soul,

Broken Prose, Spoken Poems

Health to broken hearted, words mended in
    wounded clauses,
recurring symbol in a still image—the mower
in a field made green since a month of snow melt.

This cadence—what is it it declares?
precise lines on pure white pages—
Final shining draft—polished smooth sophism,
Lovely language made lovelier
Like magnolias in May,
Conversion from death to life;

The soapy sound found in a scent of sense,
Untarnished touch of snowfall
Fallen to the coat of a wolf,
Or the yew twig's touch to human skin,
Or the tart sarcasm in the taste of tea leaves,
Labor of pain, pain in labor—

The fitting antithesis, the fleeting antipathy.

This sense in sentences—what is it it sends us?
The plummeting axe to chunks of unsplit oak,
Photo shots of words and shreds of sentences,
Perfect pictures in film of the familiar
Stuff of living;
It's the newer view in mourning, the bluer fields of
    morning.
It's the shaven face of phrases pruned, worked,
    reworded, rephrased.
It's pure moonshine obscuring the sight of stars.

THE OCEAN OF GOD

Surging heaves of house high waves roll
And leap atop each others' backs—
Whitecaps like pugnacious wrestlers in
Wind gusts rushing in furious rage,
Roaring enormous reverberations—
A tempest at its vilest!

Under this turbulent fury,
four fathoms down in
the ocean of God
sea creatures full with peace hide without fear;
thin fish swim at rest—no dread in serenity;
All's still, tranquil.

THE BELFRY TOWER BELLS

The belfry tower bell
Sends its song along the city lanes
Calling all who'll come.
The sounds resound
across the windless fields
far beyond the urban lanes.

In humid midsummer,
In frigid midwinter
The belfry tower bells
"into the highways and hedges,"
Compel all, "Come in...
that the house might be filled."

KITE

One
can feel
that fluttering
tug, rising skyward, tied in flight—
that touch like fish on a line in the fishpond.
Kite flyer eyes gaze skyward at a pliable
diamond dancing
from side to side five miles high. This aspirant
action—
this aspiration to control, curb, constrain,
command this soaring diamond
held between heaven and
earth, heard in
submissive
resistance
in currents
of winds,
or resistant
submission
to hands
that
hold
far
far
be—
low.

CLEVELAND, 28 MILES

Colors and waters of rivers—
Vermillion, Black, Cuyahoga, Huron—
Meander rambling, wayward turning,
All flow to the open palm of Lake Erie,
slowly downhill north.

On gentle swells of hills that roll to waves of this
    great lake
Between these rivers
Orchards in ordered rows sprawl,
Stretching stargrass-straight in
Unbroken pattern.

Tilled spring fields are severed only by roads,
Tree lines, long lanes reaching, leading to farm
    houses
Huddled tightly like frightened ones
hugging barns, silos, elms
fixed in these windy Midwestern fields.

Cell towers climb skyward above outstretched
    steeples
Of history. This highway, I-80 erupts in a crest
Crumpling up from the earth in
The dull rumbling growl
Of wheels rolling.

Twenty years ago in high air in the night sky
From Boeing heights, Cleveland—
Seen below—luminescent speckles like shining
    stones
Tipped, huddled in gloom against smooth shore
Far below beside Lake Erie.

THE GROUND IS SHAKING

Cobalt colored, star garlanded, blue marbled ball
swings in silence
suspending from nothing
in cerulean view from afar—
its cities fallen, risen, again and again
Over roars of wars rearing ruthless heads.
Swirling winds send cyclones round freeways of seas.
Tilted twisters twist plains. Firestorms scorch forests.
Foundations lift fault lines.
The ground is shaking.

Closer view, enclosed in meadow mist
the lake lay level in glossy brass
mirroring floating ghosts of fog,
vapors hovering like linen specters
lolling over serene veneer, lazing in fields in first
 frost ashes-
silver amid faded barn paint, fallen trees, woolen
 sheep, and stillness.
The ground is shaking.

THIRD SON

Born when we were forty
We bore crashes in crash courses: *How to Teach*
you to avert avalanches, *How to Teach*
you to include the excluded, *How to Teach*
you to hate hate.
We held our teacher's learner's permit in "all
 thumbs."
Forty when you were born, you were
Thrust into April's innocence

and incense of lilacs.
We felt small as you grew tall
In the travails of your dreams-
Dreams in dugouts and outfields,
Fish ponds and fiction books, wishes,
dreams during chorus rehearsal mornings,
idle muses, poems and songs,
deep sleep and prayers shared,
Dreams of tomorrows' maybes.
Falling to fifty, you rose to ten
Finding chapters unfolding your stories
Ones written with gentle pencils—
Rising, realizing a veiled scribe's writing.
Counting mundane seasons,
When you heard one cry above
 rumored whispers of time, "Forward!" and
You stepped into ranks of recruits.
Forward!" one bellowed.
You followed the waters of honor,
The deference of duty, doctrine of defense.
We turn sixty. You're gone.

GREEN NOVEMBER

We rush, swerve, avert crashes.
This expressway hisses in
Serpentine slowness.

Autumn crawls in late, drags her feet.
November green remains.
Nature's domain murmurs:

Too fast. Slow down.

The soul must catch the body.
Be still. Go slow.

The song of a rainbow
Raises a hue, a moment,
And is gone.

SIXTY

When we turned thirty
We spun that song long and often. Then that tune just
Stopped short
As the turntable resumed its turning
with the turn of the clock.
Today you sing "Sixty."
We recall you—on the inside sending us out-
Lunch held in hands, prayers of protection
And blessing—sending us out
To a world of broken boundaries, ruthless builders.
We recall you—on the outside pushing us in, too-
To dinner on the table, prayers of thanksgiving,
And blessing—pushing us in
From that world of broken boundaries, ruthless builders.
You spoke with the poetry of your life, still speak
Of the sometimes when it doesn't seem He answers, reciting-
"He is"—on the outside pushing us in,
On the inside sending us out.
You speak to us with poetry-
all you know of His unbroken devotion.

SLEEP

The melatonin train pulls
out of the station, rolling
slow motion somewhere
like a calm caterpillar.

This onset of slumber
Comes with dreams
In color. Shapes replace shapes.
Steam rises by summer streets.

I see souls I once knew
Burst in places I once walked.
They melt to selves I never felt,
distant spaces never seen.

I see your face on the surface of this pool–
No stir of air, blue sky behind you–
As azure as your clone is clear.
Crabs beneath hunt for crumbs.

That sure face of yours—placid echo,
That other *me* seeing me,
That look of panic we meet in dreams
Of falling, losses, foiling,

Immobile suspensions,
Frozen openness,
Recurring reveries,
Vulnerable exposure.

Stare awhile. Icy eyes see eyes,
Wake from a dream swiftly grown
To remote cold memory–
The waking—terror easing relief.

TRUCKER

Captive of coffee and the cab,
of white lines of highways—even spaced paces,
Endless dashes, bright blinks like links of chain
impeccably perpetual, trapped in this freedom—a
    prisoner.
The will to pile miles behind his eighteen wheels
drives him—forging forward
with will to outlive driven
desires to survive.

Coffee drunk through miles of years
drips in bitterness, dodging his palate. He stirs sugar,
Thinking vocally alone over twangy jangles,
banjos, oblong echoes of
pedal steel guitars in high-fidelity
country western collections.
How long lay the load of distances
between this headlong hum of tedium
and home?

At home he's Hon and Dad
Somewhere where requests for help with homework
    and
mending broken ownerships wait like patients, wait
    with patience.
Last week's welds beneath joists joining pipes—
    crawling the crawl space,
writhing, striving, soldering
alive in a grave of damp copper plumbing-
He is the firm foundation that holds it up.

Diesel pistons pump.

White lines keep passing.
Numerical clicks—odometer clamor in seclusion,
Digital ticks—clocks in lonely lonesomeness-
He hears his heart thrashing thunders.
Mountains of the western range loom ahead like
    palisades of purple.
"How long Lord...Before I go home?"

GIRL IN GOLDEN TRESSES

Starry-eyes, ears ajar-
I searched for her—this miss,
pretty in golden tresses,
And kept searching—alert-
Reciting lines of rhymed verse

Versera of the Latin denoting
"the turn at the end of a furrow with a plow."
She appears always in dreams in sleep-
There at the end of this furrow,
The edge of this field, and then

I find her where
Sun stays on golden hair, she
clasps her ashen hare, strokes
With fingers in firm forearms.
Her hare's ears fold in solace, her safe embrace.

She waits for me-
Late and long in emerald acres.
Turning at the end of that furrow-
The edge of that field,
my plow stops still, I call,

"Come, ride with me!"

Her eyes gaze, chase my face;
Irises rise, windows seek,
raising their clean emerald green
Late in the sun falling gold.

Plowing at the end of the furrow
I find the girl in golden tresses,
The miss embracing her ashen hare-
Its whiskers still, my plow still; I hear
Her voice, "I'll ride with you!"

SOMETIMES FAIRY TALES

Sometimes fairy tales are forged.
Twilight's curtains close.
Bloated moon rises in rose
from repose
Over this little city,
Waking, whitening laundered
From sleep's capricious dreams-
Eastward sitting on rooftops,
kneeling between steeples, chimneys,
Over streets where curtains close in windows,
Streets where hands hold, feet stroll.

"The moon! He's angry! In agony!"
"No. He laughs."
At dawn, whitened from sleep's capricious dreams
These two find in surprise their moon again—
Like a grouse in gray, perched in boughs,
a child's face, adrift to sleep.

THIS BLUE PLANET

Alone in a melon field the American elm
melts in summer haze.
Her hallowed tap root reaches
Down—a strong-arm longing to mingle
In bamboo,
Down, plunging toward China,
Longing—all this blue planet.
Full moon smothered in moist light
Melts in dawn mist,
sweeping across hemispheres-
Universal circuit
Circling—all this blue planet.
He dances, swirls, swinging arms of light,
Arching arms around his elm, holding her lonely
Stony heart.

VALENTINE'S DAY OWLS

Two owls
in two acmes of
tall oaks, hoot... whoo
One to the other—behind our place on
The frame of Haven's acreage. Forlorn,
Their blare—seamless meter, haunting lament,
ancient cause for caroling-
celebration—love's advent. One far, one near-
Back and forth nascent rhythm. Timbred symmetry-
Suggestive songs gesturing lyrics of primal love.
Two owls.

Two humans
in two nadirs of gravity-

We slink out to spy, visit to listen.
Limbs of white oaks like broken strings of violins
Sag from starry sky.
"Where are they?" we whisper,
Wish in darkness our presence won't offend.
Chorus to our author, hymn to their maker—our whispers, their hooting.
Flashlights scour, combing shafts through strands of branches.
Stars sparkle, dripping beams through strands of space.
We find one—a great horned—like a blessed hope
In our beam at a tree's zenith. Her heavy head
swivels, wide eyes stare, lower, glare down—our haunting luster.
Moments lurch—her perch totters.
Their lilting cadence settles to silence.
Feathers ruffle. Wings lift. She launches on silent wings.
Our light offends. Forlorn,
Two humans.

STARFISH

The tide is low; the sun is high.
They come to the end of Panmure road where
rose tinted sandbars rise above tide like backs of whales-
Large starfish—blooming bluish—
visible in tide pools—clinging to stone,
Shifting by time, slower than tide,
in no unruly hurry.

BRONX HOSPITAL

Long walk in the ICU-
Open doors—flashes of patients frayed in patient
 faces,
embraced in chains of rigid pain—grimaces—the
 same seen
one winter with frigid chills—colorless cold, seasons
 and seasons ago-
labor-frozen faces on piers on Lake Superior.

You once felt that stony snowy cold buried in the
 bones.
It's the kind of pain that blinds, howls out loud
In wordless sounds heard in
Deafening decibels, resonances,
Groans too deep for words.

YELLOW GOLD

Gulf of St. Lawrence glassy silence
Widens while we drift midway
Between islands whose calls of
Woodland ravens, crows, jays reach

Ears here—colliding from two sides
Across saltwater miles while
We fish afloat adrift on a slim craft.
Sun falls yellow-gold. The gulf

Gulls fall, cry. Under the surface
Silence of life—herring, cod, crustaceans
Crawling fathoms farther.
Mollusk shells, bones of their dead loll

Amid man's rusted ruins,
Barnacled flotsam sunken
Amid colors—as sequins-
Sea glass—white to mauve, azure

To amber, yellow-gold
Century old,
Glowing tones like
burning embers.

RUST

That tractor sat there, way out there-
Somedays seemed to stand there,
Still, in the corner of the far field, out-
where the field's edge ends near a ribbon of trees-
blurry-blue, far in the burnished haze—
a band of beeches, birches, spruces—then sky.

For some odd end, driving by,
there widened reasons to gaze
out at the bend of the field—always to see.
Somehow the tall tires have held themselves
In the dignity of wheels' ends—like shoes
immobile in the crook of the closet

under months of memories of ambles in grasses.
That tractor landed there, stayed decade after
    decade-
burning, decaying, way out there-
Cold, corroding in weather raising residual rust.
Decade after decade of dusty decay,
It told secrets it learned through waiting.

HE WATCHES US

He watches us with finished innocence,
one the sun's sparse look gives—peeking
Through a long day of low clouds—a cautious, injured look-
A glance like a bull's eye's—not cross, but armored, guarded.
He glances at us when He has no words,
Or none that would perform-
With that gaze —the one
He'd sent to Peter—their mutual moment
That last Friday-
Their cross examination.
He watches us.

LINDEN TREE

I am finally reclined. It is late afternoon.
Those likely March clouds come to smother the sun.
Wind, wool, cigar—billows of blue perfume.

My axe and sledge, saw and wedge sprawl
quiet as closed doors on the floor of the world.
I watch what the wind works to the limbs of the linden

Whose hands sway all over the sky. Imposing-
That old thing—witness to a hundred yarns, it will never befriend me.
Even in my plainest ways, it sees upheaval.

Winter will soon adjourn. By autumn these split logs—ready
For winter to come. Six decades are behind me.

I am finally reclined. It is late afternoon.

HOLLER

It's quiet-
Like parents after anger,
Or your private room after a hard, breath-losing cry.
You dream you're sledding. You stand upright
Touching a world of icy snow above a tundra which stretches
motionless miles of whiteness before you, forward, reaching...
The sled dogs are biddable, tugging, running...
Keeping you whole from whole loneliness, fleeing...
You are above, behind. They are before, minding...
You holler over frozen motionless white.

SOMEDAY

Someday when you get there you'll say "sorry"
for never saying "thank you,"
after often pleading, "please!"
to acquiescent mentors, tutors, fathers, sisters...
"sorry" for those careless assertions,
thoughtless desertions.

You took the bait—slight brown trout that you were.
They reeled you in, calmed your slimy frenzy,
Unhooked—gently as surgeons—your jaw,
Taught you forbearance,
Threw you back to the watercourse
In all its boisterous greenness.

TWENTY CITIES

Twenty cities found from printed folios
Bold and big on stained map pages
Bulge over land like growths, moles
Grown benign on human flesh.

Once little villages—all of them
Organisms that have organized
Mortals, mortar, societies of order,
All of them American—

we freely steer through,
Maneuver round, speed by on wheels.
They scarcely notice, hardly hear—
as shadowy owls' long vowels are heard.

White lights and yellow words-
Neon on rosy-orange-
Our passing is a face of headlight-eyes.
We've forty miles to the next widening city.

CATSKILL MOUNTAIN

Green moss dampness satiates darkness
down here.
Forty feet above, water
Falls
From shale ledge
in hemlock shade.
The air down here is cool.
It's not a plumb plunge-
This plummet
of water,
Like hanging rope-rain, perfect as a poem,

But a splashing
descent in prose
poured over terraces of slate,
granite, shale—
ilks of thin level stone,
forever wet,
shaded in those hemlocks
rooted in rock-
old, leaning.
This water's
forever falling
Down
Bound in gravity
Bouncing over these terraces,
Crevices, ice—froths
Always whitening in a quiet growl,
Swirling in the
Cool, cold pool
Down below
in the deep, fish-filled basin.

LAVENDER

Your favored hue, lavender-
Scarce as silver,
Loved more than blue,
Pervasive through blooms-
Tone of innocence
Scents in stillness;
Tone of devotion-
Silent, lovely,
soul cleansing lavender.

PEAR ORCHARD

In spring after winter pruning they seem
to scarcely sway, even in drafts of wind-

The pear branches with stiff gnarly
Arms, weighed in white blossoms.

They seem to stay sturdy, twisted in vigor;
the orchard's long corridors stand straight

Ascending a slight gradient rise—row on row
Planted, crafted in perfect precision—a

seamless uniform. Walks between trees
On moonless evenings depress the stars,

Sinking them low to bright nigh heights,
Hanging them like July ripe pears.

I'M HEARING YOUR BREATHING

I'm hearing your breathing.
It is early morning. You pursue the resolution—
chapters of dreaming-
a long night of sleeping.

Your breaths respire in
steady measures of life—breathing
beats of meter, distant whispers of waves-
Rhythms of breakers on the shore.

All day we strolled the coast.
Verse in wordless winds, briny sounds-
Warm water tide pools, lucidly pure-
small shell life beneath clear shallows.

You and I resume as two
Couplets in half rhyme, buds
The spring rains tussle to open,
Couplets with meter uneven,

buds that budge to blossom and blend,
couplets that struggle to synchronize,
Straining to synthesize to
a quatrain that sings.

I'm hearing your breathing.
It is early morning—one stride forward,
One blunder back—
Steady measures of life.

SPRING

Spring spills brilliant yellow, springing ajar,
dripping into April, first in flickering tints,
Then spouts of stiff daffodils, forsythias-
Like sluggish arrivals of garish stars.

We view through a new pane of glass.
Window vista unlocks layered fields of grass.
We wait to break outward like
Winter inmates held in eager fever.

There's a grand gift in the open air, and if
There's a season I could give you, I'd give you
A spring filled with spouts of stiff daffodils,
    forsythias—
Like sluggish arrivals of garish stars.

BOX TURTLE

Her shell's hard wary camouflage
full of greenish russet, ruby, pumpkin tints.
Her lower plate holds leathery yellow
Like the foot sole of a primordial warrior.
Her neck stretches, always on a threshold of
bashful retraction. She's like an army tank.
Claws dig, legs push… press in essence of mission,
expression of meekness, tedious crawling motion,
groveling serious slowness, purpose-
eggs, water, food…

Her rare arrival scarcely flashes.
Her soft-life's refinement lights with life.
We chance in happenstance.
She appears in wildflowers, weeds.
Child-like we realize she's not common stone.
Sudden surprise plunks wonder in our child-eyes,
These creatures live a hundred years.

All those decades ago—spacious pieces of past—
Rooms full of human time
form in shapes of these turtle shells-
vaults filled with stages, phases in hopes,
like coins, jewels, gold in drawers of vaults—
stock piles—charms of time
hiding in slow crawling persistence toward
 destinations—
moving always slowly forward toward some
forthcoming future—claws, legs, pressing, pushing…
pieces of time, increased dividends, securities for a
 hope chest,

Broken Prose, Spoken Poems 107

saved pieces, saved peace... "tomorrow and
    tomorrow..."
We shrink our valor in caves of fear,
Cover in safety as we hear
False alarms, traces of risk, rumbles, roaring motors,
Frights in familiar fancy.

After summer weeks without rain
Dark clouds spread west—ominous
Flashes, thunders—at last the deluge.
Gutters fill. Puddles pool in recessed grass.
Earth is hard, impeding seepage.
The surge rests; sun bursts.

Our legs push... press in essence of mission.
We walk a wet trail, reach the bridge across the creek,
come to our seventh decade.
Just ahead headstones stand like sentinels.
We stop, waver. We stroll, slower.

I'm mowing. Mundane daydreaming—then,
    surprise—
My blade hits one of these reptiles.
She was unseen, hidden, until I saw too late-
legs, head—all of her a
withdrawn introversion—remote, solitary—
held in her shell of secrecy, her ward of mystery
deceptive sense of safety inside a case of darkness
Upon her lower, leathery, yellowed plate bottom.

This engine driven blade severs her swiftly in two.
Bits of shell, greenish russet, ruby, pumpkin tints in
Blemished splashes—wet red in summer cuttings.
I close the mower's roar,

sit amid this slaughter, cover closed eyes, face,
    forehead
in open palms in summer hush. I hope she was old,
muse gloomily over our world,
this tilted, fallen sphere—waiting, ruminating...
These creatures live a hundred years.

In time I turn,
uncover the shovel, dig a shell shaped hole, scraping
    the entrails,
burying remains—this curtailed life—a turtle's verve;
then I pull the cord. The engine roars.
I finish this mundane mowing.

GRASS

We love the grass when it is dry, when water
Leaches beneath—leaving grass leaves parched
    enough to lie in-
When after brute animal day labor
we rest on our backs, or roll over
To one side, the other, then all the way over
Dozing old, full of hair like brute animals.

If we die here on this grass—these leaves combed
    thin as hair,
Maybe a loud flock of crows will see from highnesses,
Swoop low, and swallow us; or
Maybe our holder will find us, feel something, say
    something,
Then roll us into a grave—an apt interment
For old brute animals.

GOD TAKES DIRT

God takes dirt and spits in it,
puts it in my myopic eyes-
Two owlish watchers of gloom.
He breathes on me rhymes of new air.
My life-lungs open like wind.

He shoves us into a ship,
then turns away to sleep.
Thunder rumbles our tidy ease.
Our cries call in dying whispers.
He rouses. The sea sleeps.

The last Friday arrives like first frost
Silencing songs of nightingales.
Wild wolves ravage at will.
You're a passive sheep, fleeing
in weakness, hiding beneath a stone.

The Son's compliance astounds a cosmos,
fixing Himself to wood in blood.
Farsighted eyes see from afar,
Peek from weak olive grove shadows.
They hope for their old trade.

God rolls a stone with a dawn,
Steps afresh into a floral world.
His shoulders hold all of heaven;
His finger points; voice calls,
sending all who will to follow.

DAWN

Early dawn is a myth, late dawn just a story.
It's either before, or either after;
For dawn is a flash, a quick flicker, that
Flaming twinkle when sun first ascends-
Revealing all, like confessions.

Sunset too is sudden—itself under a trice
When the curtain closes fast,
Folds fully veiled. It makes a mere memorial.
That uncut present tense—its imprint—
vague, elusive, snake

Slithering—mystery swallowed,
Hidden in dim recesses of grass,
Consumed by the collision
Of yesterday, tomorrow, past and future.
It's how we live our lives—wary on what's coming.

Eyes wide on what's behind.
We stagger backward into future,
weighing where we were, stumbling, rising,
Never pausing, never still,
Never in the present, never in the current.

DUSK IN COLORADO

Look out at plum colored hills
Across a chess board of fields.
Lie back. Feel cool cobalt earth.
Breathe what the wind brings.
Hear it in the evergreens.
Unseen breezes lean on clouds.
Clouds break. Moon flickers.

Fountains of starlight spout between clouds.
Think of infinitude.
Sleep. Dream of plum colored hills.
Awaken, open, give thanks,
Hear the wind.

TOMORROW

We met this aristocrat named Tomorrow at the
    corner.
His face was serene, voice severe, brows low.
He fidgeted with fingers and a far-off smile
Advising us—just beyond the city—a bend in the path

That dips and swerves, twists further forward
through tunnels of dusky shadows
over craggy perilous ledges.
Graceful signs are staked to guide.

What unfastens after are pastures of the sun,
Galaxies of gardens of stars,
Moon shadows in shady groves,
Emerald greenness, skies and bluer seas.

We turn our backs on that anguished lady, the past-
Her fair familiar face—blemished hands
holding keys that bolt the bars of hearts.
With nowhere else to trek, we hurry forward.

SQUIRREL

Forty-five degree leaning—half uprooted, hollow-
old locust—sundry seasons—ample wood for four
    fires,
An easy cut—fifteen feet—cured, slow burning fuel.

I take my posture; chainsaw screams
until the critter—little squirrel—
peeks head and tail from the open peak
As from a door—narrow hollow home-
pleading with eyes—poor panicked tenant at her landlord,
as though crying, "Another month? My babies nestle inside."

IN WHITE RIVER JUNCTION

The Connecticut cuts into the White, two rivers
Converge in a merging graft into one,
parting Vermont from New Hampshire
where interstates transect, rails intersect,
and light stands in irremediable noon,
meeting ground between green peaks.

Luminous moon kindles
this union of moving rivers to silver fire.
Dawn's lower pasture lures hybrid bovines-
Scores of cross breeds across orchard's border.
Morphology and fog hold morning
In level rows of even trees.

Daylight rises. *Mooing* baritones lift mist to sun.
The knife of the arborist grafts new life—
Fruit mixtures, textures, living tissue in fitting *v*'s.
Between green hills in White River Junction-
This splicing of rails, rivers, roads;
This fusing of day and night; this grafting of boughs-

We sort through our lives in a grade crossing,
through our mounded memories

in our growing old, as though into
the valley of a duvet hands hold at corners.
Trains leave, bovines breathe deep cellos,
Knives cut lives, graft lives.

The sounds of rivers' whispers-
Their sea bound waters shift, flow, float
Like sails on a sea of air. Highways' sighing hisses,
falling limbs, train whistles, cows at rest—all meld.
We move away from tomorrows
in White River Junction.

DROWNING GRIEF

We grieve over the deceased
So freely we come to laugh and laugh
As though something welded within
Turns on—a sensor-mechanism opposing
emotion, a feeler to cool our fiery feeling, leveling
All our surfeiting sadness,
Drowning grief.

"Why...weep? The child... sleeps,"
He says, and those in grief laugh and laugh
After afternoon's procrastination bled into night.
One someday the long delay
Will burst open with His coming.
"Little girl, I say to you, arise,"
And we will come to laugh and laugh in great gushes
Drowning all the unfeasible grief.

SUNFLOWER

Some say the sunflower's heart can't break.
September is full of sun, hefty
Unbreakable blessedness.
They prop up heavy heads—leaning listeners-
Cheery nodding sages that love to
live like flocks, herds, packs, schools...
gregarious fields of faces that feel, consent to
refined lives of brevity.

Some say the sunflower's heart won't break.
A swift summer passes through its pithy breath of life
From planting 'til September-
When its last face flashes with life—
Blonde, leafy, brilliant fulness.
Mid-August this flower's brow lowers,
Looks downward—slow nodding frown
As though uncertain with hope.

But in September they assemble at attention-
a sea of faces in formation, as
In lower Manitoba—assembled
Full of sun, cheerful unbreakable blessedness,
Seen across miles of ceaseless horizons, waiting,
expecting... as though something is coming-
The harvester with his thresher.
Some say the sunflower's heart won't break.

DO SOMETHING

We have to do something.
We have to be heard, have something to say,
stories to tell, inventions to assemble.

Write, sing, shout, design—record breaking
Clamors of breaking sounds—
competition compelling all the world
to be heard, seen, felt.
Hands reach high crying, "Pick me! Pick me!"

The tides surge. The tides tumble.
Currents roll, flow in fluxes.
The Pacific garbage patch-
A showcase island—
augments the residual dregs of man.

GATHERINGS

Red sun rising over frozen ocean,
Sinking unflustered, slowly
Ticking, telling time.

Flocks of geese
Form formations in far fractions of sky
With destinations,

soar over lavender frost,
Their *honks* and *squeaks* acres away—cries—
Creation's urgencies, or calls

To porpoise pods in their purple struggles,
In their worlds of purposeful passages,
places of pain.

We people need each other, to hear each others' whimpers
In our gregarious creations, in our
Congregations of destinations.

A

a new apostrophe to time ..41
a time to throw away 43
a vapor 73
across the rubble of babel ...3
after a storm 6
after the hurricane 21
all afternoon 56
american kestrel 58
apostrophe to time 31
arms 17
autumn swamp maple 8

B

belfry tower bells, the 86
blue broken mussel shells .60
bluefish 40
box turtle 106
bride 20
bridges 54
broken lobster buoys 30
broken poem 63
bronx hospital 98
brown trout, woodstock, nh 46

C

catskill mountain 102
christmas night 14
cleveland, 28 miles 88
clouds of dawn, wyoming .15
conditional love 69
coyotes 1

D

dark hour 13
dawn 110
days 20
december window 10
do something 114
drowning grief 113
dusk in colorado 110

E

eastern new mexico 71
elijah 35
evangelist 50

F

first born 59
fishers island ferry view 78
flashes of memory 59
fleeing mouse 45
florida sonnet 23

G

galvanized bucket 77
gatherings 115
girl in golden tresses 94
god takes dirt 109
grand dad 48
grass 108
great horned owl 80
green eyes 19
green houses 48
green november 90
ground is shaking, the 89

H

he watches us 100
heaven's dimensions 48
hermits 5
holler 101
hurricane sandy 47

I

i dreamed you died 26

Index

i'm hearing your breathing ... 104
ice storm in new york 23
in the heart of a heatwave 10
in white river junction 112
indianapolis 74
intruders 39

K

kite 87
knolls 8

L

last season 9
late spring dogwood, new jersey 11
lavender 103
linden tree 100
long road 5

M

magic 25
maine chain link 56
march snow 36
midnight 14
mile far bonfire 42

N

new year's day 8
night of a new moon 24
nothing ever changes 12
november 4
number six dreams 62

O

october hour 24
operating room 61
order in hamden, new york 28
oriole 30

other shore, the 6

P

painting a house 16
past, the 68
pasture 57
pear orchard 104
poem for your 58th birthday 34
poet 32
poetry 84

R

rebuild 76
recesses of a summer 9
rejection 83
remember 27
road above the rivers, the . 32
rust 99

S

saints 42
sea side 53
sharon, vermont 2
shelter island autumn 34
silhouettes at sunset 72
sitting 71
six innings 46
sixty 91
sleep 92
snakes 45
snatched 82
snowfall and wool 75
sod farm meditation 70
someday 101
somehow out here 50
sometimes fairy tales 95
son 79

sound of wind, the 44	
soybean field 37	
spoken prose 64	
spring 105	
squirrel 111	
starfish 97	
stove fire 75	
summer field 47	
sunflower 114	
swans 2	

Y

yellow gold 98
yellow maples 22

T

tenses 19
terebellum shell 35
the ocean of god 86
the pardoner 77
the prodigal 11
third son 89
three ducks 11
time to prune 57
tomorrow 111
tree farm 18
trucker 93
tucson saguaro 29
twenty cities 102

V

valentine's day owls 96
vermont cemetery 17

W

waiting 54
wakefulness 40
waking from a dream 52
waterfalls 44
winter hours 55

www.ingramcontent.com/pod-product-compliance
Lightning Source LLC
Chambersburg PA
CBHW060403080526
44583CB00012B/450